THE GREATEST DECISIONS OF YOUR LIFE

GARTH COONCE

ISBN: 978-0-9777813-5-5

Published by
TCT MINISTRIES, INC.
P.O BOX 1010
MARION, IL 62959

Printed in the United States of America.

DEDICATION

This book is dedicated to the faithful partners of TCT. Your decision to support this ministry through your prayers and gifts has been a blessing to Tina, me, and our entire staff. May God richly bless you and your family.

CONTENTS

INTRODUCTION

For several years, the Lord has been impressing me to write this book.

When I look back at the turning points that brought me from a small town in Ohio to the worldwide ministry the Lord has entrusted me to lead today, I can see the hand of God at work in every step of the journey.

There were countless times when I came to a crossroads and did not know which way to turn. In those moments, I asked God to give me the courage to make the right decision—and He did!

On these pages, you will read of some "forks in the road" where we had to make choices that were extremely difficult, but necessary.

For each of the major decisions we have made, I have asked Tina to share her thoughts. As my wife and partner in ministry, she has a word from the Lord for you.

Even though the outline of this book is a reflection of personal decisions, our purpose is to inform, enlighten, and challenge you to take a giant leap of faith. Ask God to help you make choices that are centered in His will, that will cause you to enlarge His kingdom, grow spiritually, physically, materially, and in every way.

You will read about areas involving your education, your relationships, your family, and your ministry. Most important, however, is how you respond to the greatest decision you will ever make—your eternal salvation.

Please take the time to pause and reflect on what is taking place in your life today. Take an internal inventory of your heart, soul, and mind in relationship with God's vision and purpose for you. Are you listening for His guidance? Are you following His plan?

You are never too young or too old to respond to the Lord's calling.

In my case, God took a middle-aged man who was climbing high on the ladder of a major corporation, and upset my apple cart with the words, "Turn around. I have something far more important for you to do."

How will you react if God asks you to become involved in a task that seems impossible? Will you close your ears and continue down your present path, or will you respond to His voice? The Lord needs to hear from you.

I am grateful that you are taking the time to read this book. Today and tomorrow, may you make the right choices in *The Greatest Decisions of Your Life.*

– Garth Coonce

CHAPTER 1

LIFE'S GREAT DECISIONS

I'm sure, at one time or another, you've heard a friend complain, "Decisions! Decisions! What on earth am I going to do?"

Perhaps in moments of despair, you have asked that same question yourself.

One thing is for sure. You will never live one day without being faced with dozens of choices: "What should I wear?" "What will I eat? "What road should I take?"

At times, however, the decisions become much more serious:

- "Who should I date?"
- "Is this the person I am supposed to marry?"

11

- "What career path is right for me?"
- "What's the best financial investment?"

The list seems endless.

While some choices are mammoth, others are minor, but they all are important pieces in the mosaic of your life.

In this book, Tina and I will share some of the turning points we have faced during this amazing adventure. I believe you will be able to relate to many of the situations, even though every life is totally unique.

God's plan and purpose for you is different than what He has envisioned for me, but what matters most is to know we are walking in His perfect will.

SEARCHING FOR GUIDANCE

Some people go into a near-panic mode when they are faced with making a decision. I am constantly amazed at how many men and women still read their "horoscope" in the daily newspaper or online in an attempt to find direction.

Others reach out and let their fingers do the walking, phoning a trusted friend for advice, which may be "sound" or "unsound." I've also known individuals who have stopped a complete stranger and asked their opinion on a particular topic. Wow! That's really taking a chance!

There is a much better option. If they would only open the pages of God's Word, the Holy Bible, they would discover the first step to decision making. Scripture tells us, *"Trust in the Lord with all your heart, and lean not on your own understanding; in all your ways acknowledge Him, and He shall direct your paths"* (Proverbs 3:5-6).

There is a three letter word mentioned twice in the above passage that is the key to trust and direction: the word is *"all!"*

The Bible does not say we are to trust in the Lord with a fraction of our heart, but with every ounce of energy we possess, every thought of our mind, and every action we take—*"...with all your heart."* This means we are to trust God in the daily details of our lives.

The second "all" is that you are to acknowledge Him *"in all your ways..."* You may consider certain things to be insignificant, but I can assure you that they aren't to your heavenly Father. Even those problems you think you can solve on your own, they are still important to Him.

What is the reward for acknowledging God in all our ways? He will be by our side and give direction on our path. We will never, ever have a better guidance system.

God is not asking for ten or twenty percent of our time, talent, or treasure. He wants our *all.*

THE GREATEST COMMANDMENT

When Jesus walked this earth, He was constantly questioned and criticized by the religious leaders of the day. At one point, a lawyer who was a member of the Pharisees, asked Him, *"Teacher, which is the great commandment in the law?"* (Matthew 22:36).

Without hesitating, *"Jesus said to him, 'You shall love the Lord your God with all your heart, with all*

14

your soul, and with all your mind.' This is the first and great commandment. And the second is like it: 'You shall love your neighbor as yourself.' On these two commandments hang all the Law and the Prophets" (verses 37-40).

Notice how we are to love God:

- "...with *all* your heart"
- "...with *all* your soul"
- "...with *all* your mind"

The instructions from the Master could not be any clearer. We are to give God our total love.

People would have no trouble keeping the second commandment, "to love your neighbor as yourself" if they made the decision to keep the first command.

RIGHT CHOICES

Stop for a moment and consider why God inspired men to write the Scriptures. Over the centuries, on papyrus and scrolls, they carefully preserved the sacred texts so that you and I could find divine, eternal guidance and help in the decisions we make on this earth.

The Lord does not intend for us to travel this journey making choices just because we are forced to or because they are necessary; He wants us to make the *right* decisions—based on the principles He has established.

In other words, we are to make choices based on doing *right things right.* I am speaking of the actions God expects us to take in order to fulfill the plan He has designed for us.

I like what Billy Graham said on the topic: "The strongest principle of life and blessings lies in our choice. Our life is the sum result of all the choices we make, both consciously and unconsciously. If we can control the process of choosing, we can take control of all aspects of our life. We can find the freedom that comes from being in charge of our life. So start with what is right rather than what is acceptable."

If we fail to accomplish what we are placed on this earth to do, others will have to pick up the slack and make the decisions for us—and we may not like what they decide. This is why we can't ignore finishing an assignment to the best of our ability.

Why do so many start out with good intentions, stay on course for a short while, then fall by the wayside? What went wrong? Their success hinges on the thought they put into the process and the steps they take along the way.

WHAT ARE YOU SOWING?

Jesus told a wonderful parable concerning a man who went out to sow his seed (Mark 4:3-8).

- Some fell by the wayside, and the birds came and ate it.
- Other seed fell on stony ground, where it sprouted quickly, but was soon scorched because it had no sustaining root system.
- Some fell among thorns—which grew up and choked the tender plants.

But other seed fell on good, fertile ground and yielded a crop that sprang up, increased, and produced: some thirty, some sixty, and some a hundredfold.

The sower needed good judgment. Should he waste his seed by casually throwing it on the roadside, or among weeds and thorns, or should he look for "good ground" where there was a potential for a bountiful harvest?

Jesus revealed the purpose of this parable when He explained:

The sower sows the word. And these are the ones by the wayside where the word is sown. When they hear, Satan comes immediately and takes away the word that was sown in their hearts.

These likewise are the ones sown on stony ground who, when they hear the word, immediately receive it with gladness; and they have no root in themselves, and so endure only for a time. Afterward, when tribulation or persecution arises for the word's sake, immediately they stumble.

Now these are the ones sown among thorns; they are the ones who hear the word, and the cares of this world, the deceitfulness of riches, and the desires for other things entering in choke the word, and it becomes unfruitful.

But these are the ones sown on good ground, those who hear the word, accept it, and bear fruit: some thirtyfold, some sixty, and some a hundred" (Mark 4:14-20).

Although this parable was spoken centuries ago, it paints a picture of so many in today's world. Many of God's children begin their mission with hope and enthusiasm, but along the way they become side-tracked. It is obvious that the everyday busyness of life creates such pressure that their choices result in confusion and chaos.

TRADITIONS! TRADITIONS!

When Jesus looked at the decisions being made by the religious leaders in Jerusalem, His heart was troubled. In fact, He quoted from the prophet Isaiah, saying, *"This people honors Me with their lips, but their heart is far from Me. And in vain they worship Me, teaching as doctrines the commandments of men"* (Mark 7:6-7).

He went even further, calling them hypocrites, charging that by their secular choices, they were *"making the work of God of no effect through your tradition which you have handed down. And many such things you do"* (verse 13).

There is real danger on the horizon for the person who repeats the same mistakes over and over until the errors become habitual and the individual finds it almost impossible to break their addictive behavior. Jesus asked such men and women, *"Having eyes, do you not see? And having ears, do you not hear?"* (Mark 8:18).

We should not be surprised that the Bible issues this challenge: *"O you simple ones, understand prudence, and you fools, be of an understanding heart"* (Proverbs 8:5).

FROM WEAKNESS TO STRENGTH

There is a rule among carpenters that you measure twice and cut once. This is sound, professional advice. People who either fail to make a decision, or make one in haste, can set off a domino effect that will trigger many unforseen problems. In other words, their troubles multiply.

I can tell you from personal experience that it takes ten times as much effort to correct a mistake than prayerfully and carefully doing the job right the first time. Are your eyes open? Are you alert and awake? The Bible cautions, *"Watch and pray...The spirit indeed is willing, but the flesh is weak"* (Mark 14:38).

Since each of us are prone to a "weakness" problem, it only makes sense to find a "strength" answer.

This is why we cannot totally lean on our own limited reasoning powers. Instead of relying on our understanding, we are told again and again:

- *"Offer the sacrifices of righteousness, and put your trust in the Lord"* (Psalm 4:5).
- *"Some trust in chariots, and some in horses; But we will remember the name of the Lord our God"* (Psalm 20:7).
- *"To You, O Lord, I lift up my soul. O my God, I trust in You"* (Psalm 25:1-2).
- *"Trust in the Lord, and do good"* (Psalm 37:3).
- *"It is better to trust in the Lord than to put confidence in man"* (Psalm 118:8).

What does it really mean to "trust" in the Lord? You are simply saying that God is great enough and strong enough to take care of any circumstance you find yourself in. He has the wisdom necessary to give you guidance for every decision you are called on to make.

How much trust do you need to place in your heavenly Father? You are to depend on Him, *"with all your heart"* (Proverbs 3:5). This means a one hundred percent, total commitment.

FINDING THE ANSWER

On our "Ask the Pastor" program on TCT, the following question has been phoned in many times, "How can I know God's will for my life?" Or, "I have a decision to make. How can I know it is the Lord's plan for me?"

God takes great delight in pulling back the curtain of heaven and giving a glimpse of His plans and purposes to His children. He has no intention of leaving you in the dark. It may not be the entire picture, but you will begin to know what He envisions for you.

If you are committed to finding His will for your life, He will be committed to its revelation.

In the book of James, we read these words: *"If any of you lacks wisdom, let him ask of God, who gives to all liberally and without reproach, and it will be given to him"* (James 1:5).

We constantly hear from men and women who are confused about what to do regarding a specific problem—whether it is about a wayward child, a financial hardship, the death of a loved one, or other personal matters that cause pain or anxiety. It is our joy to tell them that the answer is found in God's Word.

The Apostle Paul tells us how we are to approach the Lord: *"Be anxious for nothing, but in everything by prayer and supplication, with thanksgiving, let your requests be made known to God; and the peace of God, which surpasses all understanding, will guard your hearts and minds through Christ Jesus"* (Philippians 4:6-7).

From the first verse of Genesis to the final passage of Revelation, the Bible contains the solutions for every problem.

If people would only turn to Exodus 20 and read the Ten Commandments delivered on Mount Sinai, they would come to the realization that God does not want us to lie, steal, or commit adultery. If we would just obey the first command and give the Lord first place in our lives, most of our other troubles would fade away.

LIGHT ALONG THE WAY

If you are traveling on the right road, it is easy to reach your destination. This is the benefit of opening the pages of Scripture, which have been given to us so that we will know the Father's will and the path He intends for us to follow. As the psalmist has so beautifully written, *"Your word is a lamp to my feet and a light to my path"* (Psalm 119:105).

Our responsibility, however, is to spend time in the Word, letting the Lord speak to our hearts until we have the peace and assurance that our steps are ordered from above and we are in His perfect will. If we are faithful in doing this, God will be faithful in revealing everything He desires for us to know.

Have you taken the time this week to open the inspired pages of God's Word? It holds the answers you need.

A MATTER OF FAITH

Let's face it. We live in a hurry-up, fast food, instant access world.

Unfortunately, we want God to give us answers the same way. As one fellow prayed, "Lord, please give me patience—and I want it *now!* "

There are many details about the future that the Almighty does not instantly reveal to us. If He did, what would be the purpose of belief, faith, and trust?

God doesn't always show us what will take place next month or next year. Instead, The Lord tells us again and again to live for Him by faith. *"Now faith is the substance of things hoped for, the evidence of things not seen"* (Hebrews 11:1).

Belief and trust comes first, the reality arrives in God's perfect timing.

There's a heartfelt song that is often sung on our network that was written by Ira Stanphill: *I Know Who Holds Tomorrow.* I love the words of the chorus:

> *Many things about tomorrow,*
> *I don't seem to understand.*
> *But I know who holds tomorrow,*
> *And I know who holds my hand.*

Of course, we should be concerned about the future. If you have given your heart to the Lord, you know that your eventual home will be in heaven—the place He has prepared for you. However, until that day we are to live by faith.

Paul wrote these words to the believers at Corinth: *"So we are always confident, knowing that while we are at home in the body we are absent from the Lord. For we walk by faith, not by sight. We are confident, yes, well pleased rather to be absent from the body and to be present with the Lord"* (2 Corinthians 5:6-8).

The Lord is asking us to trust Him one step at a time, day after day. As the noted pastor Oswald Smith once said, "Faith never knows where it is being led, but it loves and knows the one who is leading."

WHO IS IN CONTROL?

I was in for quite a shock when I followed God's call and left a comfortable life in the corporate world to build a Christian television station that became a worldwide network.

27

For years I had attended executive and leadership seminars that told me, "Take charge. Run the show. Don't take no for an answer. Let people know who's the boss."

Then I entered an arena where that advice was absolutely meaningless. Now I was a servant, carrying out orders that came from above. No longer was I leaning on my own understanding, but relying on the wisdom of God.

The challenges we faced were enormous, but Tina and I realized that even though we could not see the completed picture, there was One who could—God had all the facts. We only had to place our trust in Him.

Sure, the Lord gives us common sense, but that's just a small part of the answer. Without God speaking to our hearts and giving us direct revelation, our decisions can turn to disaster. This is why Scripture reminds us, *"He who trusts his own heart is a fool, but whoever walks wisely will be delivered"* (Proverbs 28:26).

Thankfully, we are in a divine partnership with a

God who is omniscient—having total knowledge. For this reason, when we trust Him in our decision-making, we are not bound by man's limitations. Hallelujah! He knows all things!

CHAPTER 2

ETERNAL DECISIONS

From my earliest recollection, I remember being in church every time there was a service—plus a whole lot more.

You could always find me enrolled in Vacation Bible School, summer camp, and I even joined the choir at one point.

At the tender age of eight, I was sitting in a service where the pastor gave a simple message on the plan of salvation, then he asked, "If you would like to accept Christ as your personal Savior, I invite you to come forward."

A force was tugging at my heart—which I now know was the conviction of the Holy Spirit—and I walked to the altar where I asked Jesus to cleanse my heart of sin. It was a wonderful moment.

However, as the years passed by, I became a busy teenager and found it harder and harder to keep my commitment.

Let me explain the conflict I faced. I had a difficult time relating to the fact that my heavenly Father truly loved me. This way of thinking had much to do with my family life.

Before I was two years old, my father left our home and I was raised by my mother and grandmother. In fact, I never saw my dad again until I was nearly 30 years old.

Because my earthly father abandoned my sister and me, the concept of a Father in heaven who truly loved me as His son didn't seem to compute.

So before long, I quit going to church and followed the path of my friends.

It was only later in life, after Tina and I were married and raising children, that my spiritual hunger increased to the point that I rededicated my life to the Lord. Without question, it was the best decision I have ever made. What's more, I found out that the love I had been missing in my wayward years had been there all along and was mine for the asking. God truly loved me—and adopted me into His family.

The more I studied Scripture, the more I realized that He had been waiting to receive me into His family all along:

> *For as many as are led by the Spirit of God, these are sons of God. For you did not receive the spirit of bondage again to fear, but you received the Spirit of adoption by whom we cry out, "Abba, Father."*
>
> *The Spirit Himself bears witness with our spirit that we are children of God, and if children, then heirs—heirs of God and joint heirs with Christ, if indeed we suffer with Him, that we may also be glorified together* (Romans 8:14-17).

Oh, what comfort, peace, and security I now have in His everlasting arms.

When Tina and I look into television cameras and

share the message of salvation, we are not uttering hollow phrases or reading from a teleprompter. Our words flow from the personal experience we have had with Jesus.

I have asked Tina to share her thoughts on the major turning points that have shaped our lives. I will let her tell you what it means to be born again.

AS SIMPLE AS A. B. C.

From Tina:

Garth and I are in total agreement that the most important decision any man, woman, or young person can ever make is to accept Jesus Christ as Lord and Savior.

This has certainly been true in our lives.

The Bible refers to this experience in various terms, such as being born-again, regeneration, salvation, and repentance. Libraries of books have been written describing what this means, which can help enlarge our understanding, but I believe it can basically be defined as a "major turnaround" from the natural ways of the world to the supernatural things of God and His righteousness.

I emphasize "His righteousness," as opposed to one's own good works, right living, or religious pursuits, because it is all based on the person of Jesus Christ—the promised Messiah, and His selfless atoning sacrifice for us on the cross of Calvary. This is revealed in Scripture with amazing detail.

Christ is the center and focus of everything: *"And the Word became flesh and dwelt among us, and we beheld His glory, the glory as of the only begotten of the Father, full of grace and truth"* (John 1:14).

In Christ is the fullness of the Godhead, the Lamb of God, Savior, Redeemer, Healer, and King of Kings.

It is only when we bow our knees to Him that we begin to fully comprehend the realities of the kingdom of God. From that point on, any wrong thinking or living begins to change in obedience to Him, and we become a brand new person. *"Therefore, if anyone is in Christ, he is a new creation; old things have passed away; behold, all things have become new"* (2 Corinthians 5:17).

Some have put it into a simple formula, as easy as A, B, C:

- Accept the Lord Jesus Christ.
- Believe in your heart that He is risen from the grave.
- Confess with your mouth, and you shall be saved.

These three steps are based on Scripture. The Apostle Paul wrote, "...*if you confess with your mouth the Lord Jesus and believe in your heart that God has raised Him from the dead, you will be saved*" (Romans 10:9).

MY HEART WAS MOVED

Whatever the process may be called, it began in my life when I was only four years old. A neighbor took my mother and me to an old-fashioned revival service at her church. Though I was not old enough to understand everything the preacher was talking about, my young mind was captivated and my heart was deeply moved. I wept at the altar, seeking to obey God the best I knew how.

Even as a young child, I believe the Lord took my decision seriously, and His hand eventually guided me to a place and people who could teach me what I needed to learn. Were it not for that early one-on-one with the Lord, I feel my life would have been a long winding road of confusion and heartache.

History clearly shows the contrast of lives: those who made the choice to turn to the light of Christ, or those who continued to cling to selfish pride and remain in darkness.

Every day that passes, I am so thankful that I found the Light of the World.

Our salvation is not a gift we receive with no output or effort on our part: it is a vital decision we must make.

A PERSONAL CHOICE

From Garth:

The reason Tina and I "invite" people to accept

Christ as we minister on TCT is because forgiveness of sin cannot be forced on anyone. It is the result of a personal choice we must make—to either accept or reject salvation.

Jesus asks for permission to enter our hearts, but whether or not we allow Him access is entirely up to us. As He declares, *"Behold, I stand at the door and knock. If anyone hears My voice and opens the door, I will come in to him and dine with him, and he with Me"* (Revelation 3:20).

This is a take it or leave it invitation. However, we had better be well informed regarding where our choices will take us.

When you boil the message down to the basics, if we make the decision to obey Christ and live a righteous life pleasing to Him, we are guaranteed an eternity in heaven. As Jesus said to His followers, *"In My Father's house are many mansions; if it were not so, I would have told you. I go to prepare a place for you. And if I go and prepare a place for you, I will come again and receive you to Myself; that where I am, there you may be also"* (John 14:2-3).

That is the good news. But what will happen to men and women who reject Christ and prefer to live in sin? According to Scripture, they are headed to an eternity of *"everlasting fire prepared for the devil and his angels"* (Matthew 25:41).

Freedom carries an enormous responsibility, and while our liberty allows us to make choices, taking the wrong road has dire consequences.

According to God's Son, our options are clear: *"He who believes and is baptized will be saved; but he who does not believe will be condemned"* (Mark 16:16).

FROM FAITH TO ACTION

Our hearts agonize over those who remain in their sin-filled lifestyles. None of us know when we will draw our last breath, and individuals who rationalize, "I'm going to sow my wild oats and wait awhile before I give my life to Christ," are playing a game far more dangerous than Russian Roulette. At any moment, our life could be over or Christ could return for His church.

39

We cannot avoid the truth that *"it is appointed for men to die once, but after this the judgment"* (Hebrews 9:27),

We also know that Christ could appear in the clouds for His church at any second. As Jesus said, *"...be ready, for the Son of Man is coming at an hour you do not expect"* (Luke 12:40). *"But of that day and hour no one knows, not even the angels of heaven, but My Father only"* (Matthew 24:36).

CAN YOU HEAR HIM KNOCKING?

While the Creator has given us the freedom to choose, we cannot escape the consequences of our choices.

Not even an Academy Award actor can fool God, no matter how hard he or she may try. "As He warns us, *"I, the Lord, search the heart, I test the mind, even to give every man according to his ways, according to the fruit of his doings"* (Jeremiah 17:10).

A person may believe that God sent His Son to earth to die on a cross for sin, but unless that individual puts faith into action, it is of no value. As James asked in the New Testament, *"What does it profit, my brethren, if someone says he has faith but does not have works? Can faith save him?"* (James 2:14). He continues, *"For as the body without the spirit is dead, so faith without works is dead also"* (verse 26).

Accepting Christ requires a decision of your mind, your heart, and your soul. The Lord may be standing at the door of your heart—gently knocking to let you know He is waiting. But He will remain outside until you answer His call and invite Him in.

ACCEPT THE GIFT

I heard the story of three preachers who were in a coffee shop discussing the topic, "When does life begin?"

Each had his own opinion. One minister commented, "I believe life begins when the child takes his or her first breath."

The second clergyman interrupted, "No—it begins

41

when the child is conceived."

The last preacher, a young, exhausted father of four, paused for a moment, smiled and said, "You're both wrong. Life begins when the last child leaves home!"

No matter where we find ourselves on life's calendar—single, married, divorced, widowed, or retired—true life begins when you come to an altar of repentance and ask Christ to wash away your sins with His precious blood. Only then do you really begin to live.

Repentance is an act of our will. Instead of continuing to follow down a path the leads to destruction, Tina and I decided to turn around and start walking with the Lord.

It can't be over-emphasized: this is a matter of choice. *"For the wages of sin is death, but the gift of God is eternal life in Christ Jesus our Lord"* (Romans 6:23).

Certainly, what Christ offers is a gift, but we must reach out, and by faith accept it. *"But as many as received Him, to them He gave the right to become*

children of God, to those who believe in His name"
(John 1:12).

YOURS FOR THE ASKING

According to surveys, the two most quoted verses in the Bible are, *"Judge not, that you be not judged"* (Matthew 7:1) and *"For God so loved the world that He gave His only begotten Son, that whoever believes in Him should not perish, but have everlasting life"* (John 3:16).

I can understand the popularity of the *"judge not"* scripture—especially when used by those who want to avoid criticism.

However, what Jesus said concerning salvation is far more profound. It has resulted in the dynamic spiritual transformation of countless millions of lives.

Many forget the setting in which these powerful words were spoken.

A Pharisee named Nicodemeus, a ruler of the Jews, came to Jesus one night, acknowledging that this "rabbi" was a teacher who had been sent from God,

"...for no one can do these signs that You do unless God is with him" (John 3:2).

Jesus brushed off the flattering remarks and came right to the point: *"Most assuredly, I say to you, unless one is born again, he cannot see the kingdom of God"* (verse 3).

Confused, Nicodemus wanted to know how a man could be born when he was old. Could he enter into his mother's womb and be reborn?"

Jesus answered, *"Unless one is born of water and the Spirit, he cannot enter the kingdom of God. That which is born of the flesh is flesh, and that which is born of the Spirit is spirit. Do not marvel that I said to you, 'You must be born again'"* (verses 5-7).

As part of that same encounter, Jesus told the man what we read in John 3:16.

This one verse speaks of:

- **The Worlds Greatest Love:** *"For God so loved the world."*
- **The World's Greatest Gift:** *"...that He gave His only begotten Son."*

- *The World's Greatest Faith:* *"...that whoever believes in Him shall not perish."*
- *The World's Greatest Life:* "...but have everlasting life."

It amazes me that something so easy is so difficult for people to accept. All we have to do is reach out and receive these amazing things. God's love is absolutely free. So is the gift He offers. The same is true of faith and life.

The price was paid by the Son of God on Calvary. It is ours for the asking.

WHAT ABOUT REPENTANCE?

There are many who misinterpret John 3:16. They read, *"whoever believes in Him should not perish but have everlasting life"* and conclude that all they have to do is to believe that Almighty God, and His Son Jesus exist. But there's more involved.

The gospel writer James corrected this when he wrote, *"You believe that there is one God. You do well. Even the demons believe—and tremble!"* (James 2:19). In other words, the devil knows the truth, yet he has not repented.

In God's kingdom, there is a direct connection between belief and behavior. Believing must be accompanied by repentance.

When Paul preached in Athens, he told the skeptics that their heathen worship of man-made idols and images was unacceptable. Paul declared, *"Truly, these times of ignorance God overlooked, but now commands all men everywhere to repent, because He has appointed a day on which He will judge the world in righteousness by the Man [Jesus] whom He has ordained"* (Acts 17:30-31).

Salvation begins with admitting that you are a sinner and asking for Christ's forgiveness: *"Repent therefore and be converted, that your sins may be blotted out, so that times of refreshing may come from the presence of the Lord"* (Acts 3:19).

MORE THAN GOOD WORKS

Some have the mistaken belief that if they do

enough good deeds, they'll make it to heaven. That's not what you'll find written in the Bible. *"For by grace you have been saved through faith, and that not of yourselves; it is the gift of God, not of works, lest anyone should boast"* (Ephesians 2:8-9).

A genuine, caring individual could go on a missions trip to Africa to help build an orphanage, serve on the board of a homeless shelter, or even give $1 million to a Christian charity, yet none of these acts will gain the person entrance into heaven. Salvation is not something to be earned, neither can it be purchased or inherited.

The Apostle Paul explained it in these terms, *"...by the deeds of the law no flesh will be justified in His sight, for by the law is the knowledge of sin"* (Romans 3:20).

There are millions who know they are deliberately living an evil life—their moral compass and guilt tells them what they are doing is wrong. Perhaps there are moments when they attempt to correct the situation, but unfortunately, their efforts are self-produced and result in no lasting change. Even more, the sin still remains in their hearts.

As the great evangelist Dwight L. Moody said, "Salvation is worth working for. It is worth man's going round the world on his hands and knees, climbing its mountains, crossing its valleys, swimming its rivers, going through all manner of hardship in order to attain it. But we do not get it in that way. It is to him who believes."

Salvation—belief and repentance—does not result from good works, but it certainly produces them. As Paul wrote to one of his converts, Titus: *"For the grace of God that brings salvation has appeared to all men, teaching us that, denying ungodliness and worldly lusts, we should live soberly, righteously, and godly in the present age, looking for the blessed hope and glorious appearing of our great God and Savior Jesus Christ, who gave Himself for us, that He might redeem us from every lawless deed and purify for Himself His own special people, zealous for good works"* (Titus 2:11-14).

In this one passage we find a progression that starts with God's grace, which leads to salvation, righteous living, looking for Christ's appearing, and doing godly deeds.

There's nothing wrong with compassion for others and selfless works, but this should be the result of a much more important decision.

Take it from one who knows: if you want to really start living, give the Lord your heart. Make sure your sins are forgiven, cast your cares on Him, and trust God with your today, your tomorrow, and eternity.

CHAPTER 3

RELATIONSHIP DECISIONS

Life has a way of taking some unexpected turns.

I graduated from high school in 1955, and the next year decided to join the United States Air Force.

After basic training, I was sent to the frozen tundra of Iceland for a one year tour of duty. It was a new adventure for me, but I was pleased when I was transferred to Hamilton Air Force Base in Novato, California—about 25 miles north of San Francisco on the San Pablo Bay.

It was a major facility during and after World War II and headquarters of the Western Air Defense Force (Hamilton was closed in the late 1970s).

I had only been there a few months when I met the love of my life. The moment I laid my eyes on her I

51

was smitten. She was beautiful, intelligent, and fun to be with—so much more than I ever dreamed or dared hope for.

After several months of dating, I decided to pluck up enough courage to ask her to be my wife. I had no earthly idea what this would entail. I really did not understand what marriage meant, but I was in love. To me, that's all that mattered.

To my delight, Tina agreed to my proposal and said YES.

I can identify with Winston Churchill who said, "My most brilliant achievement was my ability to be able to persuade my wife to marry me."

We exchanged our wedding vows on March 15, 1959, in the base Chapel with only close family and friends in attendance.

Tina was also from a broken home, and I'm sure her decision to marry was as uninformed as mine. But, thank the Lord, she had an encounter with Christ, and her spiritual commitment, prayer, and study of God's Word became the glue that held our marriage together.

As I write, we have been married 54 years and counting. While we may have made a rash decision, not knowing what our future held, the Lord certainly knew what He was doing.

In the last chapter, I stated that salvation is the most important step a person will ever take. For Tina and me, marriage holds second place.

YOUNG AND FOOLISH?

From Tina:

There is an old saying that still rings loud with truth: A woman's lot is determined by whose love she accepts.

Only heaven knows the number of women who have utterly ruined their lives—and their children's future—by choosing to marry the wrong man when they were young and foolish.

I certainly qualified for the "young and foolish" label, but because of my childhood decision to follow Christ, I believe God protected and guided me to the right man.

My heritage included many broken homes and hearts, providing me with no clue as to what true marriage should be. I lacked direction, education, refinement, talent, reputation, and good sense. Yet somehow the Holy Spirit led me to a man who would eventually provide all that and more.

Together, as partners, we would build a life and ministry that would send the Gospel to the far corners of the earth.

A BUMPY RIDE

After my all-important conversion, then came the choice who I would marry—and sticking with it!

I have to admit, however, the road wasn't always smooth; in fact the ride was rather bumpy at times. It took a firm commitment to Christ, and finding a greater purpose than ourselves. There were many days of trial and struggle when both us would have preferred an easier path.

For many years, my constant (and sometimes desperate) prayer was, "Lord, help me to be the wife that I should be."

Recently when Garth was asked how we managed to reach over 50 years of marriage, he responded, "On a scale of one to ten, with 10 being perfect, and one being awful, through the years we have hit every number!"

Today I can look back and thank God that He held our love together through it all. Unlike the famed Frank Sinatra song, both of us chose to do it "God's Way," not "My Way."

If the joy of your marriage seems a fading, distant memory, Garth and I wholeheartedly encourage you to make God the cornerstone of your home. Though an army of professional counselors and authors offer unending and well-meaning advice, Scripture provides solid wisdom for every problem, no matter how complex or seemingly hopeless—at any place, at any time.

DEFINITE DIFFERENCES

The topic of marriage is a subject about which

millions of words have been written, and countless seminars, retreats, dinners, and workshops have been held. I couldn't begin to shed all the light on the topic that is available, but let me take a moment to sum up one important principle. (In this, as the apostle Paul humbly said, "I think that I have the mind of Christ.")

I have spent previous years studying and teaching on this subject, often being invited to speak in churches by pastors who welcomed what I had to say, so let me share this with you.

It should come as no surprise that men and women are different—not just physiologically, but also emotionally and mentally. I'm sure you've heard conversations about women being more right brained (emotional) and men being more left brained (logical). Well, there is some basic truth in these findings. Not that either one is right or wrong—men and women are just wired differently.

God created the woman to be what the man needs, and vice versa! But in order for each to fulfill their particular role, we must grow into a level of maturity and selflessness, understanding our separate differences.

LOVE AND RESPECT

Just like a child, growing up takes time, often with some painful lessons learned along the way. One of the major lessons is being aware of the distinction between *love* and *respect*. God commands husbands to *love* their wives, but He commands wives to *respect* their husbands.

Why does the Lord use those two separate verbs? Aren't they pretty much the same thing? No, they are quite different. As Scripture teaches, *"Husbands, love your wives, just as Christ also loved the church and gave Himself for her"* (Ephesians 5:25). It goes on to say, *"...let each one of you in particular so love his own wife as himself, and let the wife see that she respects her husband"* (verse 33).

In general, God created woman for the nurturing and comforting role in the home, and man for providing and protecting. Women are all about emotions and feelings; in contrast, men are more focused on logic and performance. Subsequently, their inner needs are not the same.

Please don't get upset with me! I know there are always exceptions to the rules and wide variations in personalities and aptitudes. I am just offering a brief explanation of an important element to understand in the process of building a good, solid marriage.

It is generally easy for women to *love*. That is their nature. They love their children, dessert, friends, spaghetti, new clothes, and husbands. (Unfortunately, sometimes in that order.) Their deep longing is to feel adored, cherished, and secure in their husband's affection, provision, and protection.

However, the default setting in men is at the opposite end of the chart. That whole touchy–feely thing that women do is often very uncomfortable for them. They find it much easier to respect; that seems to be in their DNA.

Men look up to those who accomplish, achieve, or perform well. Some men actually respect a crook because he does his job well. Because this concept is so deeply ingrained in their being, a man's inner need is to be held in high esteem and honored—not at all the same as being loved.

I like how the Amplified Bible explains it: *"Let each man of you [without exception] love his wife as [being in a sense] his very own self; and let the wife see that she respects and reverences her husband that she notices him, regards him, honors him, prefers him, venerates, and esteems him; and that she defers to him, praises him, and loves and admires him exceedingly]"* (Ephesians 5:33 AMP).

This passage helps us understand how it is that men, often unknowingly and unintentionally, hurt a woman's feelings, while women can unwittingly make a man feel disrespected and "put down." (Note how being "dissed" has become almost an act of war to men on the street or in the hood.)

THE ONLY PLAN THAT WORKS

For a thriving, healthy marriage, each must come to realize what the other person's needs are, and choose to meet them, even though it may not come naturally.

The problem is that most of us enter into matrimony with the idea of "wedded bliss," including unrealistic expectations and demands. We think our partner's sole purpose is to make *us* happy. Whereas the reality is that we are to make *them* happy—and that takes work and commitment!

Garth and I strongly endorse the old proverb that says, "Marriages are made in heaven." If today you are struggling as a couple, don't wait another moment before turning your challenges over to the Lord. He has the only proven answers that really work.

Scripture provides solid wisdom for every problem, no matter how complex or seemingly hopeless. It has been a beacon of light for us—and I know it will be for you.

BROKEN HOMES, BROKEN LIVES

From Garth:

When I read the letters, emails, and phone call notes that pour into our TCT Prayer Centers, I am struck by the number of individuals who are praying that their relationships will be restored. It seems there are trails of broken homes and broken lives wherever we turn.

Let's face it, every union has its tense moments —and sometimes just one hurtful word said in anger can mushroom into an explosion. If left unattended and unresolved the emotional wounds will fester and may never heal.

However, regardless of how serious the matter may be, things do not have to remain as they are. Just as Christ offers forgiveness of sin, we can show compassion and forgive others, starting over with a clean slate.

If we look at the statistics, the age at which young people are entering into marriage and starting families is becoming older and older. Sadly, some look at a landscape littered with divorce and wonder if they should even marry at all.

THE "YOKE" FACTOR

When Tina and I have been asked to counsel

young people who are contemplating marriage, our first concern is that both of the individuals know Christ as their personal Savior.

We have seen the tragic results of marriages where the husband and wife are poles apart spiritually. The Word of God is emphatic on this topic: *"Do not be unequally yoked together with unbelievers. For what fellowship has righteousness with lawlessness? And what communion has light with darkness? And what accord has Christ with Belial [Satan]? Or what part has a believer with an unbeliever? And what agreement has the temple of God with idols? For you[are the temple of the living God"* (2 Corinthians 6:14-16).

According to Scripture, we are to be *"married ...only in the Lord"* (1 Corinthians 7:39).

This was true for God's people even in Old Testament days. Through Moses, the Lord gave instructions to His people concerning the inhabitants of the surrounding nations: *"Nor shall you make marriages with them. You shall not give your daughter to their son, nor take their daughter for your son. For*

62

they will turn your sons away from following Me, to serve other gods; so the anger of the Lord will be aroused against you and destroy you suddenly" (Deuteronomy 7:3-4).

I've heard all the excuses:

- "He comes from a very good background and I know He loves me."
- "She has started coming to church and I'm sure she will give her heart to the Lord once we are married."
- "I know we were raised in very different cultures and environments, but we will work this 'church thing' out."

"IN THE NAME OF LOVE"

Perhaps you've heard the phrase, "Love is blind." It certainly is when a strong believer is convinced that he or she can have such an influence on a potential spouse that the person will come to know the Lord after marriage.

I'm sure this has happened, but in my experience it is rare. The opposite usually takes place. Once the "yoke" of marriage ties the couple together, the tendency is that "in the name of love," strong faith gives way to weak faith—and you certainly know how God feels about lukewarm Christians (Revelation 3:16).

It's impossible to know how many broken hearts and sleepless nights might have been avoided if there had been some true soul-searching and prayer at the start of the relationship.

The time for evangelism is *before* marriage. However, there have been many cases where a person made a profession of faith just to satisfy their future partner, but it was only for show. When the vows were exchanged, that individual reverted back to the lifestyle they once knew.

Never rush into a union for any reason—especially with a new convert. Give that person time to demonstrate their spiritual commitment by doing what the Lord expects of every believer:

- Do they read the Word?
- Do they pray?
- Do they regularly attend the house of God?
- Do they share their faith with others?

I know that God can work miracles in lives, but when He commands that we avoid marrying saints with sinners, what is it that we don't understand?

Why risk years of unhappiness because you put your emotions first and disobeyed the Lord?

THE TRAP

We need to remember what happened to Samson, an Israelite who was perhaps the strongest man mentioned in the Bible. He made the fatal mistake of falling in love with a woman named Delilah (Judges 16:4).

She conspired with the Philistines (for money) to find out the secret of Samson's amazing strength —using every trick in the book. At one point she whispered in his ear, *"How can you say, 'I love you,' when your heart is not with me? You have mocked me...and have not told me where your great strength lies"* (Judges 16:15).

Finally, Samson buckled under her seduction and told Delilah the secret no earthly person had ever heard. He confessed, *"No razor has ever come upon my head, for I have been a Nazirite to God from my mother's womb. If I am shaven, then my strength will leave me, and I shall become weak, and be like any other man"* (verse 17).

She lulled him asleep on her lap and called for Philistine guards to cut seven locks from his hair. At that moment, as the Bible records, *"...the Lord had departed from him"* (verse 20).

He awakened to a world he was totaly unfamiliar with. It was a place with no power—no divine strength from God. What a frightening realization that must have been.

Samson had no one to blame for this but himself. If this strong man could fall into such a trap, it should serve as a warning to anyone who thinks they will be unaffected in a non-believing partnership.

AN AWESOME RESPONSIBILITY

Today society and governments are trying to impose new rules, but God set up a system that must not be changed. Jesus explained, *"Have you not read that He who made them at the beginning 'made them male and female,' and said, 'For this reason a man shall leave his father and mother and be joined to his wife, and the two shall become one flesh'? So then, they are no longer two but one flesh. Therefore what God has joined together, let not man separate"* (Matthew 19:4-6).

As Max Lucado writes, "God created marriage. No government subcommittee envisioned it. No social organization developed it. Marriage was conceived and born in the mind of God."

Yes, Jesus made an allowance for divorce in the case of an unfaithful spouse (Matthew 5:31-32;19:9), but He elevates holy matrimony to the highest possible plane—and illustrates it as a union between Himself and the church.

The Son of God tells husbands that they should

love their wives as their own bodies, because *"He who loves his wife loves himself. For no one ever hated his own flesh, but nourishes and cherishes it, just as the Lord does the church. For we are members of His body, of His flesh and of His bones"* (Ephesians 5:28:30).

This is not only a great blessing, but an awesome responsibility. As husband and wife, we demonstrate the love of Christ for each other—in sacrifice and servanthood.

The sacrifice you make in marriage is more than to each other—you are offering to God the very unity of your relationship.

THE PERFECT SPOUSE

When you think about it, marriage on earth is the closest example we have of the Lord's deep love for you and me. He promises, *"I will betroth you to Me forever; yes, I will betroth you to Me in righteousness and justice, in lovingkindness and mercy; I will betroth you to Me in faithfulness, and you shall know the*

Lord" (Hosea 2:19-20).

Like the perfect spouse, God showers His affection, care, and protection on those He loves—not to mention the gifts and favors with which He continually blesses us.

I pray you will cherish what the Lord has established—and build your home on the foundation written in His Word.

CHAPTER 4

FAMILY DECISIONS

The term "broken home," was one that Tina and I were all too familiar with. In our background there was no proven track record of a lasting marriage to emulate.

The situation became even more complex when our first child was born—a daughter we named Victoria, and called "Vicki."

She arrived several weeks early and needed to stay in a hospital incubator for a considerable length of time until she reached the weight of 5 pounds and we were able to take her home.

Because of our history, we had made a vow to stay married to each other and not subject our child to the single parent life we had both experienced. This was a real learning curve, but we were determined to follow through with our commitment.

Following my four-year obligation to the U. S. Air Force, we decided to move back to my home town in Ohio. Neither of us had any family remaining in California. While this was a rather easy decision for me, it was a difficult transition for Tina since she had always lived west of the Rockies.

UNPREPARED, BUT COMMITTED

From Tina:

After salvation and marriage, the next critical stage in our lives had to do with how we would raise our family.

For us, this was a "no brainer." Given the time period in which we grew up, anything other than total dedication to raising a child—or more than one—didn't cross our minds.

Sociologists and psychologists tell us that the first ten years of a child's upbringing shape the core beliefs that will guide his or her life. The influence of the standards and moral compass etched in their minds by that age is permanent.

Thankfully, Garth and I had been raised in an era when Judeo-Christian values were still believed and practiced in American society. I'm talking about the "old fashioned" 1940s and 50s that are so ridiculed by the young and "hip" today.

So when Vicki was born, although we were young, relatively uneducated, and immature in many ways, at least we understood that parents accepted responsibility for their children, and did the best they could to raise them.

In those days, people actually believed mothers should stay home with their children (Gasp!) unless it was truly a financial necessity to work outside the home.

When I first learned I was pregnant, I felt woefully unprepared for this new little life that would be dependent upon me. So I immediately enrolled in a local Red Cross class on "Baby and Child Care." In addition, I began devouring every book on the subject I could lay my hands on.

At that time, Dr. Spock was America's leading expert, so of course I read his popular book diligently, and subsequently studied many others through the years. One of my favorites was Robert S. Mendelsohn, M.D., who wrote, *How to Raise a Healthy Child in Spite of Your Doctor,* and *Confessions of a Medical Heretic.*

In the early days of TCT, it was a personal joy for me to interview this delightful, scholarly man in our studios. I felt he had contributed something of genuine value to our society, and his eventual passing was a loss to us all.

THE CULTURE WARS

Shortly after Vicki was born, however, in the early 1960s, it seemed the gates of hell opened, and every form of rebellion spewed forth in our society. First was the declaration that God and His silly rules were no longer welcome in the major institutions of our culture—public education, entertainment, media, and family life.

Then the Beatles, Hippies, Beat Generation, and

Bohemians, all staked their claim on a nation's consciousness. Casting off all respect for and obedience to parents—and anyone older than 30—free love, sex, drugs, rock and roll, and Eastern religions became the foundation of a counterculture that celebrated nonconformity. Rejection of their parents' values quickly spread throughout a civilization that had been based on biblical standards.

Less than ten years later, in 1973, Roe vs. Wade resulted in the Supreme Court's landmark decision to legalize abortion. The lawsuit had been filed on behalf of Norma McCorvey, who admits she had originally lied about being raped. She eventually became a member of the pro-life movement, and now supports making abortion illegal. In 1998, she testified to Congress, "It was my pseudonym, Jane Roe, which had been used to create the 'right' to abortion out of legal thin air."

What an indescribable holocaust was unleashed upon America! The recent case of the abortion provider, Dr. Kermit Gosnell in Philadelphia, has revealed only a glimpse of the bloody horrors that accompany the devaluing of children.

A DIVINE HERITAGE

In the spiritual realm, I believe it is the same evil spirit that inspired the shameful and vile practices of the heathen—which God instructed the Israelites to destroy when they entered the Promised Land after wandering 40 years in the wilderness.

One of the foremost practices was "giving their children to Baal"—the hideous ritual of placing infants in the red hot arms of the metal idol to be burned alive, while drums beat loudly to drown out their screams. How is that so different than today's practice of scalding babies alive with saline solution in the mother's womb—or virtually butchering them either a moment before or after their first breath? In many circles, the debased sexual rituals of adults are considered more important than a helpless innocent life.

In stark contrast is the Bible's beautiful declaration: *"Behold, children are a heritage from the Lord, the fruit of the womb is a reward. Like arrows in the hand of a warrior, so are the children of one's youth"* (Psalm 127: 3-4).

The Message translation presents this passage so eloquently: *"Don't you see that children are God's best gift—the fruit of the womb his generous legacy? Like a warrior's fistful of arrows are the children of a vigorous youth. Oh, how blessed are you parents, with your quivers full of children! Your enemies don't stand a chance against you; you'll sweep them right off your doorstep"* (verses 3-7).

A PARALLEL UNIVERSE

I'm so glad that Garth and I were not drawn into the evil tide that had washed over America during that time. It was like living in a parallel universe. Despite the craziness swirling around us, we just continued trying to do what we knew was right, and provide a secure home for our children.

As I mentioned, our daughter, Vicki, was born prematurely in 1959, and was sustained in an incubator until she gained enough weight to go home. Four years later, a son was also born prematurely; but he lived only two hours. It was comforting to know —as King David did—that we could not bring our little Mark back to us, but someday we would go to him.

By the time our second daughter, Julie, was welcomed into our family in 1964, my commitment to the Lord had increased dramatically. I felt my primary purpose in life was to raise them *"in the training and admonition of the Lord"* (Ephesians 6:4).

Regular church attendance and activities, as well as biblical instruction at home in every way possible became the focus of our lives. This was before the day of major Christian bookstore chains, but I was so grateful for a small local Christian bookstore where I could obtain age-appropriate resources and supplies to help "train them up in the way they should go." (See Proverbs 22:6.)

I tried to make spiritual activities fun and inspiring—like placing stars on a chart for Scripture memorization, and cute banks to save pennies for missionaries. For the kids in the neighborhood, we held Vacation Bible School and child evangelism classes in our basement.

In addition, I worked very hard at exposing our girls to intellectual and cultural pursuits as much as I was able. We were regular visitors to libraries, museums, stage plays, concerts, and planetarium shows at the local university. Even though family funds were extremely limited, we managed to include a few additional classes in drama, music, dancing, and art.

As the girls grew older, they graduated to sports and church youth group activities, until finally the time came when we were able to send them both to Oral Roberts University, which we felt was the finest Christian school in the country.

ON THEIR OWN

It was in Tulsa that Vicki and Julie found their husbands-to-be, and we were comfortable in releasing their care to the fine young men they chose. Our dedication to them and their families continues to this day. Both girls now have families of their own; and Vicki even has grandchildren! But we are still the patriarchs of our family, and remain fiercely committed to their welfare.

As all parents, however, we have to admit that we have undoubtedly failed them many times along the way through our human weakness, ignorance, and misunderstanding. We thank God they have always forgiven and continued to love us.

These days, we have to smile to see them struggling with some of the same issues with their children as we did in their early years. I enjoy wickedly telling them often, "The purpose of grandparents is to spoil children, and protect them from their parents!"

WORDS OF WISDOM?

From Garth:

I'm not the first to admit that parenting is not a bed of roses. It can bring out our strongest attributes, and our weakest.

I once heard of a pastor who gave a talk about

parenting—even before he had a child. His title was, "How to Raise Your Children."

Then he and his wife became parents of a baby boy. It was quite a while before he gave that talk again, but when he did, he changed the title to, "Suggestions for Struggling Parents."

As time passed, he and his wife added two more children to their family. Once more, he changed the title of his talk to, "Hints for Hopeless Parents."

Finally, when they became teenagers, he opened his parenting speech with, "Does anyone here have a few words of wisdom?"

THE OWNER'S MANUAL

Paul's teaching to the believers at Ephesus gives us counsel and advice on how to establish the kind of relationships God expects us to have with our children. He writes, *"[I] beseech you to walk worthy of the calling with which you were called, with all lowliness and gentleness, with longsuffering, bearing with one another in love, endeavoring to keep the*

81

unity of the Spirit in the bond of peace" (Ephesians 4:1-3).

We often talk about the importance of children obeying their parents, but what about parents nurturing and raising their sons and daughters?

Whenever I buy a new computer or a car, it comes with a detailed owner's manual, but not so with kids. However, there is a resource you can turn to that will give you all the wise counsel needed concerning raising strong, loving children: God's Word.

For example we are told, *"Fathers, do not provoke your children, lest they become discouraged"* (Colossians 3:21). In other words, bite your tongue, pray for patience, and don't fly off the handle!

God also gives us specific instructions: *"These words which I command you today shall be in your heart. You shall teach them diligently to your children, and shall talk of them when you sit in your house, when you walk by the way, when you lie down, and when you rise up. You shall bind them as a sign on your hand, and they shall be as frontlets between your eyes. You shall write them on the*

doorposts of your house and on your gates"
(Deuteronomy 6:6-9).

A WORD TO DADS

It's so easy for fathers to assume that because they are good providers, their mission is complete. Some have the mistaken notion that the mother has the primary responsibility for raising children.

No, it's a partnership.

Allow me to share a dose of advice from Dr. James Dobson: "A Christian man is obligated to lead his family to the best of his ability. If his family has purchased too many items on credit, then the financial crunch is ultimately his fault. If the family never reads the Bible or seldom goes to church on Sunday, God holds the man to blame. If the children are disrespectful and disobedient, the primary responsibility lies with the father—not his wife."

He continues, " [Our] greatest need is for husbands to begin guiding their families, rather than pouring every physical and emotional resource into the mere acquisition of money. Fathers, God wants us to be directly involved in the lives of our children. We cannot delegate it to our wives."

To that I say, "Amen!"

UNCONDITIONAL LOVE

One of the most powerful lessons I have ever learned was to make certain that the love we have for our children is unconditional.

I've observed parents who shower their sons and daughters with love as a reward, only to withdraw it as punishment. Such treatment leads to tremendous insecurity for the child.

I am convinced that your children will not remember you primarily for the "goodies" you showered on them as they were growing up. They will take far more comfort in the fact that you were there for them in the midnight hour when their tummy ached, or when you helped them glue and paste together their third grade school project. They'll think of how you held them tightly in your arms, praying with them and letting them know how much they were loved and cherished.

As Charles Swindoll points out, "Each day of our

lives we make deposits in the memory banks of our children"

The mom or dad who brushes their kids aside while rushing through the day are communicating a message that screams, "You are not my priority."

I agree with those who say, "Our children spell "love" as "T-I-M-E."

Parental love must be a constant presence —dependable, life sustaining, and always there. If God's heart is overflowing with never-ending love for His children, so should ours. Our heavenly Father *"is merciful and gracious, slow to anger, and abounding in mercy"* (Psalm 103:8). He assures us, *"I have loved you with an everlasting love"* (Jeremiah 31:3).

As parents, can we do any less?

WHAT ARE THEY WATCHING?

From the beginning of TCT, we have felt the burden and responsibility to provide wholesome, God-honoring children's programming on our network. For years, we have scheduled a 6-hour block of Saturday morning shows especially targeted for young people.

Now, because of the help of our partners, this outreach is greatly expanding. Our separate channel, TCT KIDS, is now available 24 hours a day, 7 days a week.

The statistics of birth are astounding. In the next 24 hours more than 370,000 babies will be born worldwide. Next year, in the United States and Canada alone, over four million new children will become citizens.

As we have shared, Tina and I know what it's like to raise kids—and the importance of making sure the input they receive in their formative years will give them a strong and lasting foundation. Research tells us that the average 4-year-old asks over 300 questions every day! That's not only impressive, it places a huge responsibility on moms and dads.

According to Nielsen research, the average child spends over four hours daily watching television in its various forms (including mobile devices and the Internet).

What are they watching? Sadly, the vast amount of programming comes from writers and producers whose moral standards are far different than believers.

As a result, young, impressionable minds are being bombarded with scenes of alcohol, drug use, and casual sex being painted in a positive light. Plus, they are exposed to countless mind-numbing hours of violence and filthy language.

Someone recently asked, "Why are you showing a children's program at two o'clock in the morning? Aren't kids supposed to be sleeping?" They forget that this channel is being watched worldwide. The middle of the night in New York is afternoon in Bangkok and Manilla.

THE NEXT GENERATION

Let me encourage you to tell your friends, especially those with children in the home, to watch TV KIDS. There are numerous ways to receive it! Along with DirectTV and DISH satellite systems; if you live in a city with a local TCT station, you can receive all four of our channels off air. Those with ROKU can also get all four channels (and even newer devices are now being developed). Or, if it's not available on your cable system, you can simply go to www.tct.tv on your computer, and click on "Watch TCT," then click on "TCT Kids." Even easier is adding the free TCT Mobile App to your phone or tablet! For iPhone, iPad, and iPod, click on the App Store. For Android devices, download at Google Play.

Why are we putting so much effort into building this channel into a viewing destination that is inviting and exciting? We sense the urgency and know the value of sharing divine principles with the next generation.

Even at very young ages, boys and girls want to know, "What on earth am I here for?" This is why our objective is to focus on God-centered content, sound doctrine, age-appropriate basic Bible knowledge, and the practical application of truth.

From the letters and emails we receive, moms and dads are grateful that we are spending such time and effort on this channel.

WHAT TRULY MATTERS?

As the Apostle Paul wrote to Timothy, *"From a child you have known the Holy Scriptures, which are able to make you wise for salvation through faith which is in Christ"* (2 Timothy 3:15).

We pray this will be repeated in the lives of millions of young people. Our desire is to see the words of the prophet Isaiah fulfilled: *"All your children shall be taught by the Lord, and great shall be the peace of your children"* (Isaiah 54:13).

Far more important than a child's abilities in math, science, athletics, art, or music, is the question of their soul's salvation. I heard someone say, "What would it profit a man to gain the world and lose his family?"

Jesus is still saying, *"Let the little children come to Me, and do not forbid them; for of such is the kingdom of heaven"* (Matthew 19:14)

The Great Commission includes hearts of all ages.

CHAPTER 5

EDUCATIONAL DECISIONS

When people take an introspective look to determine the momentous decisions of their lives, they realize that not all journeys are the same.

For most individuals, the order starts with education, then moves to career, marriage, children, etc. Hopefully, there will be a major spiritual commitment at some point along the way. But in my case, education came later—after our two children had been born.

In the U.S., it is expected that young people graduate from high school, so what I am referring to is a college level education, with a particular career goal in mind.

A turning point for me took place in 1966 when

the U.S. Congress passed the Veterans Readjustment Benefits Act. Prior to that time, the G.I. Bill (The Servicemen's Readjustment Act of 1944), provided educational benefits only for those who had served in wartime. Now it was expanded to include veterans who had been in the military during periods of both war and peace.

The benefits were generous—low cost home mortages, low-interest loans to start an enterprise, cash for college tuition and living expenses.

Immediately, I made the decision to enroll in college with the objective of receiving a degree in accounting and economics. It was a five-year program, but I was convinced I could accomplish the necessary requirements in four years by attending summer classes.

I also knew that I had to support our family, so I continued my full time employment. Tina was behind my decision all the way.

In the process, I landed a job as a press operator for a major corporation and kept that position for the next two years. Then, in 1968, I was given a promotion to production manager and held the title until I finished college and received my Bachelor of Science degree.

After graduation, I was offered a transfer to be the controller of our company's largest plant—in Chicago. We made the decision to move to the Windy City with our two daughters.

This was all in God's plan, since it led us to a wonderful church and pastor where I became grounded in my faith, grew very strong in the Lord, and received the infilling of the baptism of the Holy Spirit.

AN AMAZING AGENDA

From Tina:

When God opened the door for Garth to pursue a college degree, it was part of His blueprint to place us into a position for what He was calling us to do. We didn't realize it at the time, but He had an amazing agenda planned—including both our educational and spiritual preparation.

Garth, growing up in a small Ohio community,

certainly knew the meaning of hard work. He also realized that opportunities were extremely limited where he lived. That's why, after graduating from high school, he pursued the most logical path available to him, joining the military—and working in electrical power production at Air Force bases.

When his tour of duty for Uncle Sam ended and we were married with a child, we returned to Ohio. Garth continued to practice the only way of life he understood—hard work and accepting responsibility. At times, this meant juggling two jobs to provide for our small family.

So when the expanded G.I. Bill offered assistance for education, he jumped at the chance to improve himself and our lives. At the start, he enrolled in daytime classes at the local university—and took a job as a night watchman, which enabled him to study between rounds. Then came his career advancements.

HIDDEN WISDOM

Although Garth doesn't like to toot his own horn,

I'm proud to say that his natural intelligence and aptitudes enabled him to learn even complex subjects quickly and graduate with high grades.

Later he would go on to earn his Masters and Doctoral degrees, along with a few honorary degrees bestowed on him for his significant work in Christian ministry.

As other faithful wives have done, helping with writing papers and being both mother and father to the children, I like to think I earned my "PHT" degree (Putting Hubby Through)!

His educational progress resulted in promotion to better assignments, and he insisted that it was now time for me to go back to school, utilizing his textbooks which were still current, rather than waiting until the children were older, and having to buy new ones.

By now, I had learned to appreciate the value of education, and loved the college studies. But my main occupation was mother and wife, so I was a part time student for many years. When our daughters were grown I was finally able to attend full time, and am grateful for the things I learned that have enabled me to be more effective in ministry.

For followers of Christ, however, the most meaningful knowledge you will ever receive is found written in the pages of God's Word. As the Bible states, *"Study to show thyself approved unto God, a workman that needeth not to be ashamed, rightly dividing the word of truth"* (2 Timothy 2:15).

In Christ are hidden all the treasures of wisdom and knowledge—just waiting to be discovered.

I encourage you to strive for excellence in everything possible, taking advantage of any opportunity to grow, expand your horizons, and open your heart to become a more effective ambassador for Christ. This may include taking classes at your church, a local community college, on-line courses, volunteering at a worthwhile organization, or immersing yourself in the works of God-ordained authors of our day.

In the process, take the words of Scripture seriously: *"Whatever your hand finds to do, do it with your might"* (Ecclesiastes 9:10).

AN AVALANCHE OF INFORMATION

From Garth:

I'm sure you have heard the term "information overload." That's a valid description of today's world of instant communication—with billions of bits of data being stored on computer chips as small as a pinhead.

If you study God's Word, you will understand that this was prophesied long ago as a sign of the last days. The Lord told Daniel that at *"the time of the end; many shall run to and fro, and knowledge shall increase"* (Daniel 12:4).

The avalanche of information is mind-boggling—and it is multiplying at a geometric rate. According to current research:

- Computers become twice as smart every 18 months.
- The amount of new technical information is doubling each year.
- Researchers add 2,000 pages to man's scientific knowledge every minute.

97

- The material produced by scientists in a 24-hour period would take one person five years to read.
- Over 3,000 new books are published daily.
- Every day, the equivalent of over 300 million pages of text is transmitted via the Internet.
- The number of text messages sent and received every day exceeds the population of the planet.
- It is estimated that one week's worth of articles in *The New York Times* contains more information than a person was likely to come across in a lifetime in the 18th century.
- It has been projected that in just a few short years, the average personal computer will exceed the computational capabilities of the entire human species.

NEW TECHNOLOGY

At TCT, we are fully aware of the knowledge explosion and realize that how and where people receive our programs is rapidly changing. This is why, with the help of our partners, we have expanded far beyond delivering the message of Christ into homes simply from our stations and through satellite or cable networks.

Today, people around the world can watch all four of our channels streaming live on the Internet. This includes TCT, TCT Family, TCT Kids, and La Fuente, our Spanish language channel.

All this makes it possible for us to reach the 2.7 billion Internet users worldwide. Hourly, people are clicking onto our programs in Bangladesh, Pakistan, United Arab Emirates. Saudi Arabia, Iraq, Egypt, Finland, Vietnam, Ghana, Zambia—and over 100 nations.

Talk about knowledge being increased! The number of people who can watch our four channels has skyrocketed as a result of developing technology. As we mentioned in the last chapter, cell phone and tablet apps allow people to view TCT on mobile devices (for free!), and TCT can be streamed from the Internet to television via ROKU and similar players. Gone are the days when people had to be at home in front of a television to be able to watch their favorite programs.

KNOWLEDGE FROM ABOVE

I believe that every man, woman, and child should try to acquire as much education as they possibly can; but unless it includes knowledge of both God's earth and heaven, they will become unbalanced in their thinking.

How can we profess to be truly enlightened if we ignore the eternal principles established in Scripture? As the psalmist wrote, *"Forever, O Lord, Your word is settled in heaven"* (Psalm 119:89). Remember, Jesus declared, *"Heaven and earth will pass away, but My words will by no means pass away"* (Matthew 24:35).

The most acclaimed scientists can propose theory after theory of how this world came to be, but until they recognize the hand of the Creator, their search will forever be in vain.

The very first verse in the Bible says it all: *"In the*

beginning, God created the heavens and the earth" (Genesis 1:1). We can analyze, theorize, and extract tons of facts and data about the planet on which we live, but unless this is linked with revelation knowledge that comes from above, our education is not complete.

Look up! "The heavens declare the glory of God; and the firmament shows His handiwork" (Psalm 19:1).

The primary objective of TCT is to present the simple message of Christ to the unsaved, on whatever continent they may live. In the process, we believe the Holy Spirit accompanies everything we do—and that's what makes all the difference. You see, "The natural man does not receive the things of the Spirit of God, for they are foolishness to him; nor can he know them, because they are spiritually discerned" (1 Corinthians 2:14).

The person who attempts to drive a wedge between human knowledge and the things of God will never completely understand the universe the Almighty created.

101

We cannot afford to turn a blind eye to the source of all truth. *"For the Lord gives wisdom; from His mouth come knowledge and understanding"* (Proverbs 2:6).

King Solomon, a man of great wisdom and riches, made this statement: *"Apply your heart to instruction, and your ears to words of knowledge"* (Provebs 23:12).

A FOUNDATION FOR LIFE

The British evangelical theologian, John R. W. Stott, wrote, "Knowledge is indispensable to Christian life and service. If we do not use the mind that God has given us, we condemn ourselves to spiritual superficiality, and cut ourselves off from the many riches of God's grace....Knowledge is given to us to be used, to lead us to higher worship, greater faith, deeper holiness, and better service."

Spiritual knowledge is not just for the church, it should be the foundation for all endeavors—even government. Our first president, George Washington, made this profound statement: "It is impossible to rightly govern the world without God and the Bible."

INSIGHT AND WISDOM

The knowledge that comes from above is the bedrock wisdom for us personally, and it gives us the ability to teach others. From the Amplified Bible, here is what the Apostle Paul wrote to the Colossians: *"Let the word [spoken by] Christ (the Messiah) have its home [in your hearts and minds] and dwell in you in [all its] richness, as you teach and admonish and train one another in all insight and intelligence and wisdom [in spiritual things, and as you sing] psalms and hymns and spiritual songs, making melody to God with [His] grace in your hearts"* (Colossians 3:16 AMP).

No life is fully equipped without the insight and training that comes from a study of Scripture. As Paul wrote to young Timothy:

But you must continue in the things which you have learned and been assured of, knowing from whom you have learned them, and that from childhood you have known the Holy Scriptures, which are able to make you wise for salvation through faith which is in Christ Jesus.

All Scripture is given by inspiration of God, and is profitable for doctrine, for reproof, for correction, for instruction in righteousness, that the man of God may be complete, thoroughly equipped for every good work (2 Timothy 3:14-17).

IS IT RELEVANT?

Non-believers in and out of academic circles keep asking the question, "Why do these Christians place so much trust in a book that was written thousands of years ago? How could it possibly be relevant today?"

Little do they realize that a Living God wrote a Living Book. It reveals both His love for this world, and His plans for man's future.

Those who take the time to find out, are usually surprised to discover that the Bible is either quoted or alluded to in literature and world history more than any book ever written.

- God's Word is above human experience: *"For we did not follow cunningly devised fables when we made known to you the power and coming of our Lord Jesus Christ, but were eyewitnesses of His majesty. For He received from God the Father honor and glory when such a voice came to Him from the Excellent Glory: 'This is My beloved Son, in whom I am well pleased'"* (2 Peter 1:16-17).

- God's Word is above human traditions: Jesus asked the scribes and Pharisees, *"Why do you also transgress the commandment of God because of your tradition?"* (Matthew 15:3).

- God's Word is above human knowledge: *The fear of the Lord is the beginning of knowledge"* (Proverbs 1:7).

- **God's Word is above human wisdom:** *"Has not God made foolish the wisdom of this world? For since, in the wisdom of God, the world through wisdom did not know God, it pleased God through the foolishness of the message preached to save those who believe"* (1 Corinthians 1:20-21).

- **God's Word speaks with authority:** *"In the beginning was the Word, and the Word was with God, and the Word was God....And the Word became flesh and dwelt among us, and we beheld His glory, the glory as of the only begotten of the Father, full of grace and truth"* (John 1:1,14).

PRINCIPLES AND PROMISES

Some look at the Ten Commandments and scornfully say, "The Bible is just a bunch of do's and don'ts. Far from it. Scripture contains principles and promises for positive living. Instead of confining us in

106

a box of restrictions, it tells us how we can freely conduct our lives in the image of God and His Son, Jesus Christ.

The prophetic words of Scripture *"never came by the will of man, but holy men of God spoke as they were moved by the Holy Spirit"* (2 Peter 1:21).

The students in our major universities are being taught by professors who have the luxury of unlimited facts and research at their fingertips, but many still avoid or skirt the truth. It's always, "Well, it might be," or "I'm not really sure if this is true or not."

Paul the Apostle warned that this would happen at the end times. He wrote, *"But know this, that in the last days perilous times will come: For men will be... always learning and never able to come to the knowledge of the truth"* (2 Timothy 3:1-2,7).

What is the reason for this? They *"resist the truth"* (verse 8). Paul described the situation that sounds just like today when men and women *"will turn their ears away from truth, and be turned aside to fables"* (2 Timothy 4:4).

This must break the heart of God, *"who desires all*

men to be saved and to come to the knowledge of the truth" (1 Timothy 2:4).

Until the last trumpet sounds, *"The Lord is...not willing that any should perish but that all should come to repentance"* (2 Peter 3:9).

WHATEVER HAPPENED TO THE WORD?

One of the reasons our network has a focus on the teaching of God's Word is because today's houses of worship are a far cry from the first century church we read about in the New Testament.

Where are most pastors missing the mark? They are not giving members of their congregations the pure, unadulterated knowledge of God. Instead, they speak about social issues, community needs, or offer a "feel good" message that is nothing more than positive thinking with a couple of scriptures thrown in for good measure.

The words of the prophet Hosea are as true today as when he wrote them: *"My people are destroyed for lack of knowledge"* (Hosea 4:6).

What will it take to bring spirit and life back to our churches, our families, and our nation? *"Preach the word! Be ready in season and out of season. Convince, rebuke, exhort, with all longsuffering and teaching"* (2 Timothy 4:2).

GRADUATION DAY IS AHEAD

I earnestly pray that you will develop such a passion for the study of God's Word that it will become as necessary to your existence as the air you breath. The psalmist expressed it this way: *"As the deer pants for the water brooks, so pants my soul for You, O God. My soul thirsts for God, for the living God"* (Psalm 42:1-2).

In a society that is hungry for position, power, and prestige, the eyes of the Lord are searching the earth for people who have an insatiable appetite for Him.

The more time we feast on His Word, the more our hearts, souls, and minds will be satisfied.

Jesus tells us, *"I am the bread of life. He who comes to Me shall not hunger, and he who believes in*

Me shall never thirst" (John 6:35).

It is exciting to be on a journey that not only leads to the knowledge and wisdom of the Lord, but prepares us for the ultimate graduation ceremony —when we will be given a crown of righteousness and enter the gates of the eternal city.

A "HIGHER" EDUCATION

Without question, a quality education is a necessity for career development, financial security, and contributing to society. However, to unlock the true riches of life—peace of mind, a pure heart, and a satisfied soul—we need a "higher" education—one that comes from God Himself through the instructions inscribed in His eternal Word.

I pray that your eyes have seen and your heart has received what the Lord has written in the Ultimate Textbook.

CHAPTER 6

MINISTRY DECISIONS

B eing raised in a Christian home and regularly attending Sunday School and church, were part of my early upbringing. However, being totally transparent, as a young man, and into my business career, I had more questions than answers concerning spiritual matters— and I slowly drifted away from the things of God.

The focus of my life became climbing the corporate ladder and taking care of Tina and our two beautiful daughters.

Even when my wife rededicated herself to the Lord and was growing in faith by leaps and bounds, I was reluctant and held back—attempting to

111

somehow build a wall between myself and what truly mattered.

It was only after seeing the amazing transformation in Tina, that I began attending church with her. At the time, I had no earthly idea what the Lord was planning for both of us.

The Apostle Peter addressed this topic in the New Testament when he wrote, *"Wives...be submissive to your own husbands, that even if some do not obey the word, they, without a word, may be won by the conduct of their wives, when they observe your chaste conduct accompanied by fear [of the Lord]* (1 Peter 3:1-2).

Tina was God's hand extended and her example caused me to make a fresh commitment to the Lord —one that proved to be both permanent and life-changing.

After finding a Spirit-filled church where the Word was preached in depth, we made tremendous spiritual strides. The day eventually came when Tina and I were teaching "Life in the Spirit" seminars. Parallel with this, God was seriously dealing with me about my future.

"WHY NOT YOU?"

If you have read some of my earlier books, you know what took place on Thanksgiving weekend, 1976. For those who may be new to the story, let me briefly summarize what happened.

Tina and I were attending a regional convention of the Full Gospel Business Men's Fellowship International in Cincinnati. It was there that I opened up and shared with my wife what God had been impressing on my spirit. I confided in her, "I feel God is speaking to my heart concerning a new ministry He wants us to lead."

I had no clue of any details—only that God was at work in our lives.

During the years we had lived in Youngstown, Chicago, and Cleveland, we were pleased that a few Christian programs for children were aired on local stations. We felt it was a positive influence on our children as well as countless others. Now we had moved to Cincinnati, and those programs were not being shown there.

The Lord began dealing with my heart concerning the situation. Whether I was awake or asleep, I constantly heard His words, "Instead of seeking a few good children's programs here, why don't you build a Christian television STATION for Me?"

Although I knew what it took to be a corporate executive, I had absolutely no confidence in my ability to start a non-profit media venture. As a result, I was having a rather tough time staying committed to the idea.

However, as the months passed by, all doubts were swept away as I realized it truly was God speaking into my life. My belief and enthusiasm grew to the point I could no longer contain my excitement and I declared to all who would listen what was about to happen.

One verse surged through my mind over and over again: *"...being confident in this very thing, that He who has begun a good work in you will complete it"* (Philippians 1:6).

A DIFFICULT DECISION

As a result of what took place that Thanksgiving weekend, I made the decision to pursue this God-inspired vision. Without question, it was a giant leap of faith.

I knew this would greatly impact our family life. Our daughters were maturing, going to college, getting married, and having our wonderful grandchildren.

My response to God's vision, and my commitment to His directive to build a Christian television station was not a passing whim. I submitted myself totally to His will—and surrendered my entire future to His calling.

The above Scripture that reads, *"...He who has begun a good work in you will complete it,"* had been a foundational verse to me through the years.

During the early days, in practically every conversation, I would share that verse. It reached the point that when I started speaking, my friends took great delight in beating me to the punch—quoting the words of the scripture before I even had a chance to say them!

And God *was* doing a work! It would take turbulent years of constant prayer and perseverance —even when some thought we had lost our minds. Tina and I are living testaments to the fact that what God ordains, He sustains.

UNCHARTED WATERS

From Tina:

The final critical decision of our lives was, as it is sometimes called, "entering full-time ministry."

I had been extremely proud of Garth, who spent more than two decades in corporate life and rose to a very responsible position that took him to exciting international locations. Obviously, it would be a major jolt to his system to leave all that behind and sail into unknown and uncharted waters.

Garth knew God was leading him to establish a Christian television station, but he still had a few doubts and constantly asked "Why me?" He didn't know anything about television, but we knew people who did!

The Lord could have called any of them; but His answer was unmistakable: "I chose you *because* you don't know anything about it. If you did, you would do it your way. But you will have to trust Me—every step of the way. And if you do, some day you will look back and be amazed at what I have accomplished through you."

At the time, being involved in God's work was not anything new to us. Garth had been active in the Full Gospel Businessmen's Fellowship, taught Sunday School, the "Life in the Spirit" seminars he mentioned earlier, and we had led numerous home Bible studies for several years.

For me, from the moment I committed my life to Christ, my entire focus had been about ministry. Serving the Lord, studying the Word, sharing the Gospel, and building up others in the faith was a "grand obsession."

Of course, being a wife and mother was my

foundation and identity; but early on, my pastor wisely insisted that I begin conducting adult Sunday School classes. The weekly study and preparation began a lifetime habit of Bible teaching, ministry to, and discipling of other women—no matter where I was or how I might otherwise be employed.

AN ADDED DIMENSION

Over the years, this continually expanded in the various places we lived. So for me, going into full time Christian television was just an added dimension of what I had been doing for years.

However, as that joy and outreach had grown, so did greater challenges. I can now identify with many others in ministry—especially those in the field of Christian broadcasting—that everything I thought I knew would eventually be sorely stretched, turned inside out, shaken together, pressed down, and running over. As I recently told a friend, "...run over by trucks!"

It seems the "prince of the power of the air"

doesn't like anyone messing with his atmosphere, and the devil launches massive, well-armed and devious attacks on those who dare to put the Gospel into the airwaves. That's when we learn from hard experience that *"the weapons of our warfare are not carnal but mighty in God for the pulling down of strongholds"* (2 Corinthians 10:4).

The biblical pattern is that all followers of Christ are "in the ministry," regardless of how they earn a living. We think of the Apostle Paul as being a great missionary, but he supported himself as a tent-maker (Acts 18:3).

Scripture details that God established certain positions in the church—apostles, prophets, evangelists, pastors, teachers—not for *them* to do all the work of the ministry themselves, but rather, *"for the equipping of the saints for the work of ministry, for the edifying of the body of Christ"* (Ephesians 4:12). Furthermore, the Bible tells us that we are to *"walk worthy of the vocation wherewith ye are called"* (Ephesians 4:1 KJV).

SALT AND LIGHT

Jesus instructed us to go into the whole world, proclaiming the Gospel, and being salt and light. He explained:

> *You are the salt of the earth; but if the salt loses its flavor, how shall it be seasoned? It is then good for nothing but to be thrown out and trampled underfoot by men.*
>
> *You are the light of the world. A city that is set on a hill cannot be hidden. Nor do they light a lamp and put it under a basket, but on a lampstand, and it gives light to all who are in the house.*
>
> *Let your light so shine before men, that they may see your good works and glorify your Father in heaven* (Matthew 5:13-16).

As most people know, salt adds and intensifies flavor, improves the quality of life, and preserves from decay and corruption. Light enables people to see and find their way in the midst of confusion and darkness.

This is what believers in Christ are called to be in every situation, as they spread out into nations and societies.

The intention of Almighty God is that the followers of His Son would influence and make an impact as they come in contact with unbelievers, causing them to "see" and "thirst" for the Living Water and life of Christ.

For this reason, Christians who separate themselves into cloistered or communal lifestyles really do not fulfill God's purposes. I have seen directories of "Christian Yellow Pages," which may be well-meaning, but to me, they are contrary to what the Lord has in mind.

To borrow a phrase: *How dost thou know, oh man, if thou needest a plumber, and an unbelieving plumber journeys to thy tent to repair thy pipes, thou mayest become a witness to him of the goodness of God. But if thou callest only a Christian plumber, who then can witness to the unbelieving plumber?*

121

LASER-LIKE INTENSITY

For both or us, founding and operating a Christian television network called deeply upon our years of experience and focused it into laser-like intensity—often utilizing everything we had ever learned, while at other times teaching us things we never wanted to know. There have been unbelievable joys and mountain tops, along with deep and dark valleys that threatened to destroy us. But through it all, one thing has never wavered—our commitment to Jesus Christ, and more importantly, His faithful commitment to us.

We have spent over 50 years walking with Him, with 35 of those in the ministry of Christian television, and He has never let us down, in spite of our mistakes and sometimes abject failures.

Today we have the added blessing of seeing our children and grandchildren with an anointing resting on their lives and a calling to continue this marvelous work.

BEHOLD! BEHOLD!

I can say with all honesty we have tried to do exactly what the Lord has called us to do for such a time as this—to proclaim the marvelous Good News of His love with the strength of a voice amplified through electronics. As Isaiah 40:9 says so eloquently: *"O Zion, you who bring good tidings, get up into the high mountain; O Jerusalem, you who bring good tidings, lift up your voice with strength, lift it up, be not afraid; say to the cities of Judah, "Behold your God!"*

That is what Christian broadcasting does: it proclaims to the cities of the world, "Behold your God!"

- Watch what the Lord does through this ministry.
- See Him in this program, in that program.
- Hear what He says through that pastor.
- Be blessed by His music through this singer.

- Watch Him use that skilled musician, or athlete.
- Receive His wisdom through this teacher.
- Understand the times through that prophet.
- Rejoice as He calls sinners to repentance through this anointed evangelist.
- Learn about the good work He established through that apostle.
- Praise Him as He heals a man or woman with no hope.
- See how He gloriously changed lives from fear and darkness to joy and everlasting light.

On and on, around the clock, people can "Behold their God." They can see His mighty works as Savior, Healer, Baptizer in the Holy Spirit, and Soon Coming King.

Behold your God—the promised Messiah, Redeemer, Risen Son of God, Second Person of the Godhead, the Word Become Flesh—in Him dwells all the fullness of the Godhead bodily. For Him and by Him all things were created and exist. It's all

about Him! He is all of this and more! His name is
Jesus.

Behold your God!

YOU HAVE A MINISTRY

From Garth:

If you have given your heart to the Lord and made
a commitment to walk with Him, you have a ministry
too.

As believers, we are not called to simply warm a
pew or just watch a Christian television program. The
Bible tells us we are to *"be doers of the word, and not
hearers only"* (James 1:22).

The Bible speaks of *prophets* (who represent God
to the people) and *priests* (who represent the people
to God). When you study the Old Testament, you
find that only a very few, the priests, had access to
the Almighty in the sacrificial process. But starting
with the New Covenant, every believer is now a
priest unto God: *"You are a chosen generation, a
royal priesthood, a holy nation, His own special*

125

people, that you may proclaim the praises of Him who called you out of darkness into His marvelous light" (1 Peter 2:9).

No longer do we have to sit outside and wait for a priest to enter the Holy of Holies in the Ark of the Covenant. We now have been given *"boldness to enter the Holiest by the blood of Jesus, by a new and living way which He consecrated for us, through the veil, that is, His flesh"* (Hebrews 10:19-20).

I trust you realize that your very body, *"is the temple of the Holy Spirit who is in you, whom you have from God"* (1 Corinthians 6:19).

Praise the Lord!

YOUR DIVINE ASSIGNMENT

Like infants who must learn to crawl before they can walk, it is only natural for new Christians to wonder, "What is my purpose in God's kingdom. What role does the Lord expect me to play?"

I can assure you of this: every believer, from the time they are first saved—whether a housewife, a teenager, a business person, or a minister of the Gospel—has been given one overriding assignment. We are called to be *"ambassadors for Christ"* (2 Corinthians 5:20).

You have been divinely appointed by the King (Jesus Christ) to represent Him everywhere you go.

In addition, God has nine specific gifts available to believers:

[To] one is given the word of wisdom through the Spirit, to another the word of knowledge through the same Spirit, to another faith by the same Spirit, to another gifts of healings by the same Spirit, to another the working of miracles, to another prophecy, to another discerning of spirits, to another different kinds of tongues, to another the interpretation of tongues. But one and the same Spirit works all these things, distributing to each one individually as He wills" (1 Corinthians 12:8-11).

127

We each have a ministry to perform—inside the walls of the church and outside in the world. Please ask God to commission and empower you to fulfill that assignment—whatever it may be.

At TCT, we have prayer partners whose primary mission it is to bring the needs of our viewers to the Lord through intercessory prayer. What a wonderful calling.

Today, it is my prayer that you have found your place, your niche, your particular avenue of service to the Lord.

CHERISH YOUR GIFT

God's Word tells us, *"As each one has received a gift, minister it to one another, as good stewards of the manifold grace of God. If anyone speaks, let him speak as the oracles of God. If anyone ministers, let him do it as with the ability which God supplies, that in all things God may be glorified through Jesus Christ, to whom belong the glory and the dominion forever and ever"* (1 Peter 4:10-11).

128

The body of Christ will only remain strong if *"every part does its share"* (Ephesians 4:16).

What an honor and privilege to be ministering in the great harvest field. Please take this moment to say, "Thank you, Lord, for the opportunity you have given me. Please bless my service—and may You receive all the glory."

CHAPTER 7

THE CHOICE IS YOURS

As a young boy, being raised by my mother and grandmother, I looked around and saw people who had far more material possessions than our family was able to afford.

I came to the conclusion that I had three choices: (1) to be content with my lot in life, (2) complain about what I didn't have, or (3) I could do whatever was necessary to eventually have what I wanted.

Even at the tender age of eight or nine, I began watching successful men and women very carefully —making mental notes on what they did and how they worked to achieve their goals.

It's not that I coveted what belonged to them, rather I wanted to know what it would take to see my own dreams come true. What effort would be required on my part?

I refused to be unhappy and focus on what I *didn't* have, but set my heart on what I *could* have. I made a decision to see my future, not my present situation.

As a teenager, I promised my mother, "One day I am going to buy you a house of your own"—and I reminded her of this many times.

Of course, that seemed out of the realm of possibility in our current circumstances. Mom just smiled and said, "I'm sure you will"—not really believing it would ever happen.

However, the last 20 years of my mother's life she lived in the house of her dreams because God blessed me and I was able to buy her what previously had been unattainable.

I also made many rash promises to my new bride that seemed immature and far-fetched at the time, yet today, those dreams have all been surpassed.

I learned a valuable lesson. Our tomorrows are created by the decisions we make today. The past cannot be lived over again, the present only lasts for a moment, but the future is forever.

There is no limit to what we can accomplish through faith in God. We may look at a problem, become overwhelmed, and cry out, "No way!" But remember, the Lord sees beyond our human vision. In the words of Jesus, *"With men this is impossible, but with God all things are possible"* (Matthew 19:26).

THE ULTIMATE CHOICE

The sun will rise one morning when you can no longer rest on your laurels, but will have to make a decision that will affect your future. I'm not referring to the kind of home you will buy or the car you're thinking about driving. Rather, the choice is the biggest one you will ever make: how will you will spend eternity?

One of the most significant moments in the history of the children of Israel took place after Joshua crossed the Jordan River and possessed the Promised Land

There had been a series of mighty battles, starting with Jericho. It took many years before the Israelites were able to subdue its enemies and claim the territory.

Joshua, now near the end of his life, called all the tribes together—elders, chiefs, judges, and officers. Then he spoke to them in what was essentially a farewell address: *"I am old, advanced in age. You have seen all that the Lord your God has done to all these nations because of you, for the Lord your God is He who has fought for you"* (Joshua 23:2-3). This was an up-and-coming generation of Israelites; the older leaders had died during the wanderings in the wilderness.

As part of his speech, he cautioned concerning the dangers of living with unbelievers: *"You shall not make mention of the name of their gods, nor cause anyone to swear by them; you shall not serve them nor bow down to them, but you shall hold fast to the Lord your God"* (verses 7-8).

So they would not repeat the mistakes of the past and forever remember the greatness of Jehovah God, Joshua then reminded them of the entire history of Israel—from the days of Abraham, Isaac, and Jacob to Moses being sent to Egypt to free their ancestors from the bondage of Pharaoh.

He reviewed the plagues, the miracle of the parting of the Red Sea, and how God protected them in the wilderness. Then Joshua told them to abandon the gods their ancestors idolized in Egypt and worship the one and only true Living God.

Finally, he brought them to a place of decision —and asked them to make a choice that is as relevant today as it was thousands of years ago. Joshua issued this challenge: *"Choose for yourselves this day whom you will serve, whether the gods which your fathers served that were on the other side of the River, or the gods of the Amorites, in whose land you dwell. But as for me and my house, we will serve the Lord"* (Joshua 24:14-15).

NOT TOMORROW, BUT TODAY!

What an awesome challenge! This was not a suggestion to mull over and make tomorrow or at some more convenient time in the future. Joshua demanded that they decide immediately: *"this day!"*

We all have a choice to make:

135

Adam and Eve had to make a decision:

Would they listen to God—who told them they would die if they ate of the Tree of the Knowledge of Good and Evil? Or would they fall for Satan's smooth talk, who told them just the opposite: *"You will not surely die"* (Genesis 3:4).

Unfortunately, they made the wrong choice.

Noah had to make a decision:

Without a drop of rain in sight, would this old man build an ark on dry ground and become a laughing-stock? Or would he listen to the voice of the Lord?

"By faith Noah, being divinely warned of things not yet seen, moved with godly fear, prepared an ark for the saving of his household" (Hebrews 11:7).

Abraham had to make a decision:

Would he stay in the land of his birth surrounded by his loved ones, or respond to God, who told him, *"Get out of your country, from your family and from your father's house, to a land I will show you"* (Genesis 12:1)?

The Bible records, *"By faith Abraham obeyed when he was called to go out to the place which he would receive as an inheritance. And he went out, not knowing where he was going"* (Hebrews 11:8).

Through Abraham, the nations of the world were blessed.

Moses had to make a decision:

When God spoke to him at the burning bush, Moses could have either stayed tending his sheep, or follow the instructions of the Almighty and return to Egypt for a task that seemed impossible.

Moses obeyed the Lord and led the Israelites out of Egypt—after 430 years of bondage (Exodus 12).

Jonah had to make a decision:

The Lord spoke to Jonah, saying, *"Arise, go to Nineveh, that great city, and cry out against it; for their wickedness has come up before Me"* (Jonah 1:2). Would he listen to God?

No, Jonah headed for Tarsus. It took the experience in the belly of a whale before he finally obeyed the Lord and preached in Nineveh—where the city was saved.

Peter had to make a decision:

This disciple denied the Lord three times, but after the resurrection, Jesus asked Peter to follow Him once more, telling him to *"Feed My lambs," "Tend My sheep," "Follow Me"* (John 21:15,16,19).

After the outpouring of the Holy Spirit on the Day of Pentecost, it was Peter who preached in Jerusalem and 3,000 souls were saved (Acts 2:41).

Paul had to make a decision:

On the road to Damascus, where it was his objective to harass followers of Christ, Saul (later Paul) was blinded by a light from heaven and heard the voice of Jesus say, *"Saul, Saul, why are you persecuting Me?"* (Acts 9:3).

He could have cursed God and remained in his sin, but instead he made a choice that not only affected his future—but continues to impact millions who read the New Testament. Trembling, Paul replied, *"Lord, what do You want me to do?"* (verse 6).

Jesus had to make a decision:

Before the crucifixion, when Jesus was arrested and was about to be brought to trial before the Sanhedrin, He asked the disciples this significant question: *"Do you think that I cannot now pray to My Father and he will provide Me with more than twelve legions of angels?"* (Matthew 26:53).

The choice Jesus made, however, was not based on His personal feelings, but so that Scripture might be fulfilled. In the Garden of Gethsemane, He prayed, *"Father, if it is Your will, take this cup away from Me; nevertheless not My will, but Yours, be done"* (Luke 22:42).

WHAT IS YOUR DECISION?

Jesus chose the humiliation and suffering of being nailed to the cross, where He shed His precious blood so that you and I can come to Him and receive forgiveness of sin. He paid the ultimate price for our salvation.

Christ died and was buried. But, thank God, on the third day He rose from the grave. Today, He is with

His Father in heaven, ready to make intercession with God on your behalf.

It is the will of your heavenly Father that you find forgiveness of sin, but the choice is yours. You can either accept or reject God's offer of redemption.

Today, Tina and I pray that you will make the greatest decision of your life—to receive Christ as your personal Lord and Savior.

May you rejoice and say with, Joshua: "For me and my house, we will serve the Lord!"

BOOKS BY GARTH COONCE

HOW TO KEEP YOUR LIFE IN FOCUS
THE MIRACLE OF TOTAL COMMITMENT
A VOICE, A VISION, A VICTORY

BOOKS BY TINA COONCE

LIFE IN THE RIGHT SEAT
FOR WOMEN ONLY

To Contact the Author
or to Learn More About TCT:

TCT Ministries
P.O. Box 1010
Marion, IL 62959

Phone: 618-997-9333
U.S. Prayer Center: 313-534-1818
Internet: www.tct.tv
Email: correspondence@tct.tv